# LIFE|EXPLORED

## WHAT'S THE BEST GIFT
## GOD COULD GIVE YOU?

### HANDBOOK

**Life Explored Handbook**
Copyright © 2016 Christianity Explored
www.life.explo.red

Published by:
**The Good Book Company Ltd**
Blenheim House, 1 Blenheim Road, Epsom, Surrey, KT19 9AP, UK
Tel: 0333 123 0880; International: +44 (0) 208 942 0880
Email: info@thegoodbook.co.uk

**Websites:**
UK and Europe: www.thegoodbook.co.uk
North America: www.thegoodbook.com
Australia: www.thegoodbook.com.au
New Zealand: www.thegoodbook.co.nz

CHRISTIANITY
**EXPLORED**
MINISTRIES

ISBN: 9781784980825

Design by André Parker

Printed in India

# CONTENTS

# WELCOME TO
# LIFE|EXPLORED

We all want to be happy. Over the next seven sessions, we'll explore some of the ways we try to find that happiness, and ask the question, "Are we looking in the right place?"

**Key**

▷ Watch a film

≡ Discuss a question

📖 Read a Bible passage

# SESSION 1
# THE GOOD GOD

▷ Overture Part 1

≡ What's the best gift God could give you?

27 *God created mankind in his own image,*
    *in the image of God he created them;*
    *male and female he created them.*

28 *God blessed them and said to them, "Be fruitful and*
*increase in number; fill the earth and subdue it. Rule over the*
*fish in the sea and the birds in the sky and over every living*
*creature that moves on the ground."*

29 *Then God said, "I give you every seed-bearing plant on the*
*face of the whole earth and every tree that has fruit with seed*
*in it. They will be yours for food.* 30 *And to all the beasts of*
*the earth and all the birds in the sky and all the creatures that*
*move along the ground – everything that has the breath of life*
*in it – I give every green plant for food." And it was so.*

31 *God saw all that he had made, and it was very good.*

Genesis 1:27-31

---

**Blessed** | Looked on them with          **Subdue** | Bring order to.
love and promised good things.

---

## ▷ Overture Part 2

- Human beings have been described as "the glory and the garbage" of the universe.

- We're "glorious" because we're made by a glorious God, who has made us "in his own image" (Genesis 1:27).

- Being made "in God's image" means that we can know and enjoy this God. God wants us to enjoy him!

- We flourish most, and enjoy him best, when we reflect him best.

- But there's the "garbage" too. Rather than enjoying and reflecting our Creator, we enjoy and reflect "created things" more. We have other "gods".

- A person's "god" is anything they cling to and rely upon for their ultimate security and contentment.

¹ *The heavens declare the glory of God;*
*the skies proclaim the work of his hands.*
² *Day after day they pour forth speech;*
*night after night they reveal knowledge.*
³ *They have no speech, they use no words;*
*no sound is heard from them.*
⁴ *Yet their voice goes out into all the earth,*
*their words to the ends of the world.*
*In the heavens God has pitched a tent for the sun.*
⁵ *It is like a bridegroom coming out of his chamber,*
*like a champion rejoicing to run his course.*
⁶ *It rises at one end of the heavens*
*and makes its circuit to the other;*
*nothing is deprived of its warmth.*

⁷ *The law of the LORD is perfect,*
*refreshing the soul.*
*The statutes of the LORD are trustworthy,*
*making wise the simple.*
⁸ *The precepts of the LORD are right,*
*giving joy to the heart.*
*The commands of the LORD are radiant,*
*giving light to the eyes.*
⁹ *The fear of the LORD is pure,*
*enduring forever.*
*The decrees of the LORD are firm,*
*and all of them are righteous.*
¹⁰ *They are more precious than gold,*
*than much pure gold;*
*they are sweeter than honey,*
*than honey from the honeycomb.*

Psalm 19:1-10

**Glory** | God's perfect and limitless goodness.
**The LORD** | Literally *Yahweh*, the name of God.

**Statutes, precepts, decrees** | Rules/laws.
**Righteous** | Right in God's eyes; perfectly good.

1. According to verse 1, the heavens and the skies are telling us something. What is it?

2. When and where can that message be heard, according to verses 2-4?

3. Let's take a look at verse 4. It says, "God has pitched a tent for the sun". What do you think we're being told here about what God is like?

4. From verse 7 onwards, the writer begins talking about "the law of the LORD", the Bible. What do verses 7 and 8 say about God's words, and the effect they will have on us if we listen to them?

5. Think of the popular views many people have about God. How does the God we've seen in Genesis 1 and Psalm 19 differ from these?

**6. If you knew Psalm 19 was true, how would it affect the way you feel about God?**

**7. (If time) What has been most striking for you during this session?**

**Note:**

For more on the subject of the Bible, visit **www.life.explo.red**

# SESSION 2
# THE TRUSTWORTHY GOD

▷ **Hotel Part 1**

🗨 **What's your current view of God, and how did you reach that viewpoint?**

*¹Now the serpent was more crafty than any of the wild animals the* LORD *God had made. He said to the woman, "Did God really say, 'You must not eat from any tree in the garden'?"*

*² The woman said to the serpent, "We may eat fruit from the trees in the garden, ³ but God did say, 'You must not eat fruit from the tree that is in the middle of the garden, and you must not touch it, or you will die.'"*

*⁴ "You will not certainly die," the serpent said to the woman. ⁵ "For God knows that when you eat from it your eyes will be opened, and you will be like God, knowing good and evil."*

*⁶ When the woman saw that the fruit of the tree was good for food and pleasing to the eye, and also desirable for gaining wisdom, she took some and ate it. She also gave some to her husband, who was with her, and he ate it.*

Genesis 3:1-6

---

**Crafty** | Deceitful.
**Garden** | The Garden of Eden.

**Your eyes will be opened** | You will understand new things.

---

## ▷ Hotel Part 2

- What if the God we don't believe in, or the God we don't trust, isn't actually the God revealed in the Bible?

- Adam and Eve rejected God because they believed a lie about him: they thought they would be happier and more fulfilled without him.

- We too reject God when we believe that making someone else (or something else) our ultimate authority will be better for us.

- God's response to Adam and Eve's rejection is his response to ours. There's judgment: we face death. But he also pursues us in love, offering a rescue from the death we deserve.

- That rescue would involve God himself entering the world, suffering and even experiencing death. He would take our punishment, so that we don't have to.

- Would you trust God if you knew he loved you enough to give up his life for you?

[book icon] [18] The wrath of God is being revealed from heaven against all the godlessness and wickedness of people, who suppress the truth by their wickedness, [19] since what may be known about God is plain to them, because God has made it plain to them. [20] For since the creation of the world God's invisible qualities – his eternal power and divine nature – have been clearly seen, being understood from what has been made, so that people are without excuse.

[21] For although they knew God, they neither glorified him as God nor gave thanks to him, but their thinking became futile and their foolish hearts were darkened. [22] Although they claimed to be wise, they became fools [23] and exchanged the glory of the immortal God for images made to look like a mortal human being and birds and animals and reptiles.

[24] Therefore God gave them over in the sinful desires of their hearts to sexual impurity for the degrading of their bodies with one another. [25] They exchanged the truth about God for a lie, and worshipped and served created things rather than the Creator – who is forever praised. Amen.

Romans 1:18-25

---

**Wrath** | God's settled anger against sin.
**Divine** | Of, from, or like God.

**Degrading** | Shaming; dishonouring.

---

1. How does verse 25 say people treat God?

2. What kinds of things do we "worship and serve" rather than God?

3. How are people described in the passage?

4. We might say, "But what about people who've never heard of God, or people who think he doesn't exist?" How does this passage – and Psalm 19 from the last session – speak to that question?

5. Look again at your answer to question 3. How does God respond to this, according to verse 18?

6. Do you feel that's fair of God? Why or why not?

**7. (If time) What has been most striking for you during this session?**

# SESSION 3
# THE GENEROUS GOD

▷ Gold Part 1

≡ What keeps you going in difficult situations?

¹ *The* L*ord* *had said to Abram, "Go from your country, your people and your father's household to the land I will show you.*

² *"I will make you into a great nation,*
 *and I will bless you;*
*I will make your name great,*
 *and you will be a blessing.*
³ *I will bless those who bless you,*
 *and whoever curses you I will curse;*
*and all peoples on earth*
 *will be blessed through you."*

Genesis 12:1-3

**Abram** | Later, God changed Abram's name to Abraham.

**Bless/blessing/blessed** | Generously given good things by God.

## ▷ Gold Part 2

- We sometimes think of God as being demanding. But he's overwhelmingly generous.

- God promised that through a man called Abraham, "all peoples on earth will be blessed" (Genesis 12:3). In other words, the "garbage" we see in the world would one day be fixed by one of Abraham's descendants.

- God doesn't choose who to bless based on where a person has come from, what they have (or haven't) done, or what they look like.

- As the story of Abraham and Sarah shows, receiving God's blessings doesn't depend on human effort or ability at all.

- By contrast, the "gods" we tend to live for instead are extremely demanding in terms of human effort.

- The promise to Abraham – that all peoples on earth would be blessed – is fulfilled in Jesus Christ.

*[1] Jesus entered Jericho and was passing through. [2] A man was there by the name of Zacchaeus; he was a chief tax collector and was wealthy. [3] He wanted to see who Jesus was, but because he was short he could not see over the crowd. [4] So he ran ahead and climbed a sycamore-fig tree to see him, since Jesus was coming that way.*

*[5] When Jesus reached the spot, he looked up and said to him, "Zacchaeus, come down immediately. I must stay at your house today." [6] So he came down at once and welcomed him gladly.*

*[7] All the people saw this and began to mutter, "He has gone to be the guest of a sinner."*

*[8] But Zacchaeus stood up and said to the Lord, "Look, Lord! Here and now I give half of my possessions to the poor, and if I have cheated anybody out of anything, I will pay back four times the amount."*

*[9] Jesus said to him, "Today salvation has come to this house, because this man, too, is a son of Abraham. [10] For the Son of Man came to seek and to save the lost."*

Luke 19:1-10

---

**Jericho** | City near the Jordan river.
**Sinner** | Someone who sins by breaking God's laws.
**The Lord** | Jesus.

**Salvation** | Being saved from sin.
**Son of Abraham** | From Abraham's family line (i.e. Jewish).
**Son of Man** | A title Jesus often used for himself.

---

1. Zacchaeus was a wealthy tax collector who worked for the Romans. He would have been seen as a parasite, getting rich by working for the enemy. What "god" do you think Zacchaeus was living for (verse 2)?

2. Given Zacchaeus' reputation, how were the crowd expecting Jesus to treat him (verse 7), and what is the big shock of verse 5?

3. What effect does this have on Zacchaeus, according to verse 6? What evidence is there that Zacchaeus no longer worships the same "god" he did before he met Jesus (verse 8)?

4. Religion says, "If you're a good person, God will accept you." What's remarkable about what happens here in verses 5-8?

5. In verse 3, Zacchaeus is looking for someone. In verse 10, Jesus ("the Son of Man") says he's looking for someone as well. Who is he looking for and why?

6. If you knew that God related to you the way that Jesus related to Zacchaeus, how would you feel?

7. (If time) What has been most striking for you during this session?

# SESSION 4
# THE LIBERATING GOD

▷ **Lawn Part 1**

≡ Often we feel our lives would be complete "if only" we had someone or something. What's your "if only"?

⬚ *⁷ The* Lord *said, "I have indeed seen the misery of my people in Egypt. I have heard them crying out because of their slave drivers, and I am concerned about their suffering. ⁸ So I have come down to rescue them from the hand of the Egyptians and to bring them up out of that land into a good and spacious land, a land flowing with milk and honey – the home of the Canaanites, Hittites, Amorites, Perizzites, Hivites and Jebusites. ⁹ And now the cry of the Israelites has reached me, and I have seen the way the Egyptians are oppressing them. ¹⁰ So now, go. I am sending you to Pharaoh to bring my people the Israelites out of Egypt."*

Exodus 3:7-10

**The** Lord | Literally *Yahweh*, the name of God.
**Canaanites, Hittites, Amorites, Perizzites, Hivites and Jebusites** | Groups of people who lived in the area of Canaan.
**Oppressing** | Persecuting and mistreating.
**Pharaoh** | King of Egypt.

## ▷ Lawn Part 2

- Jesus said, "Everyone who sins is a slave to sin" (John 8:34). The history of the Israelite slavery in Egypt points towards the way in which we can be freed from our slavery to sin.

- God sent a series of plagues against Egypt because they'd enslaved and abused his people for 400 years. Eventually, God warned Egypt that if they refused to free the Israelites, the firstborn son in every family would die.

- As a reminder that the Israelites had also sinned and deserved judgment, God warned that this plague would affect them too.

- But there was a way out. They would be spared if the blood of a lamb was put on the doorframes. The lamb died in their place.

- This moment in history pointed towards the much greater liberation that Jesus would one day provide on the cross: he would die in our place. That's why Jesus was called "the Lamb of God" (John 1:29).

- When we put our trust in him, we are freed from the penalty our sin deserves. We're also freed from the power sin has over us, because our "if onlys" are transformed.

*27 [Jesus said,] "All things have been committed to me by my Father. No one knows the Son except the Father, and no one knows the Father except the Son and those to whom the Son chooses to reveal him.*

*28 "Come to me, all you who are weary and burdened, and I will give you rest. 29 Take my yoke upon you and learn from me, for I am gentle and humble in heart, and you will find rest for your souls. 30 For my yoke is easy and my burden is light."*

Matthew 11:27-30

**Committed** | Handed over; entrusted.
**Yoke** | A wooden crosspiece placed across the neck of two animals and attached to the plough or cart they are to pull.

1. What remarkable things does Jesus say in verse 27 about his relationship with God the Father?

2. In verse 27, Jesus says that no one can know God the Father except those Jesus reveals him to. Do you feel it's arrogant of Jesus to make that claim? Why or why not?

3. Verse 28 is an invitation to everyone who feels weary and burdened. Given your own experience, and what we've heard in this session, what kinds of burdens do you think Jesus might be talking about?

4. Jesus said he came to give his life "as a ransom for many" (Mark 10:45). What does a "ransom" have to do with Jesus' death?

5. In verse 29 Jesus says, "Take my yoke upon you". What would you say to someone who said, "I'm not becoming anyone's slave!" What kind of master is Jesus, according to verses 28-30?

6. What would it feel like to serve a master like this – one who died to set you free?

7. (If time) What has been most striking for you during this
   session?

# SESSION 5
# THE FULFILLING GOD

▷ **Geisha Part 1**

≣ **What are you hoping will bring you fulfilment in life?**

*⁶ Jesus, tired as he was from the journey, sat down by the well. It was about noon.*

*⁷ When a Samaritan woman came to draw water, Jesus said to her, "Will you give me a drink?" ⁸ (His disciples had gone into the town to buy food.)*

*⁹ The Samaritan woman said to him, "You are a Jew and I am a Samaritan woman. How can you ask me for a drink?" (For Jews do not associate with Samaritans.)*

*¹⁰ Jesus answered her, "If you knew the gift of God and who it is that asks you for a drink, you would have asked him and he would have given you living water."*

*¹¹ "Sir," the woman said, "you have nothing to draw with and the well is deep. Where can you get this living water? ¹² Are you greater than our father Jacob, who gave us the well and drank from it himself, as did also his sons and his livestock?"*

*¹³ Jesus answered, "Everyone who drinks this water will be thirsty again, ¹⁴ but whoever drinks the water I give them will never thirst. Indeed, the water I give them will become in them a spring of water welling up to eternal life."*

John 4:6-14

---

**Samaritan** | From Samaria. Jews and Samaritans hated each other.
**Jacob** | Abraham's grandson.

**Eternal life** | Perfect, sinless life that lasts forever in the joyful presence of God.

---

### ▷ Geisha Part 2

- We're richer than we've ever been – we have more leisure time, more freedom and more opportunity – yet many of us feel less fulfilled than ever. Why?

- Many of us seek fulfilment anywhere but in the place we were designed to find it: in God himself.

- Except perhaps for a short time, other sources of fulfilment don't satisfy. They weren't intended to. "All our dreams come false."

- In the Old Testament, God identifies himself as "the spring of living water", the one who satisfies our deepest thirst for fulfilment.

- In the New Testament, Jesus identifies himself in the same way: "Whoever drinks the water I give them will never thirst. Indeed, the water I give them will become in them a spring of water welling up to eternal life" (John 4:14).

<sup>14</sup> "After he had spent everything, there was a severe famine in that whole country, and he began to be in need. <sup>15</sup> So he went and hired himself out to a citizen of that country, who sent him to his fields to feed pigs. <sup>16</sup> He longed to fill his stomach with the pods that the pigs were eating, but no one gave him anything.

<sup>17</sup> "When he came to his senses, he said, 'How many of my father's hired servants have food to spare, and here I am starving to death! <sup>18</sup> I will set out and go back to my father and say to him: Father, I have sinned against heaven and against you. <sup>19</sup> I am no longer worthy to be called your son; make me like one of your hired servants.' <sup>20</sup> So he got up and went to his father.

"But while he was still a long way off, his father saw him and was filled with compassion for him; he ran to his son, threw his arms round him and kissed him.

<sup>21</sup> "The son said to him, 'Father, I have sinned against heaven and against you. I am no longer worthy to be called your son.'

<sup>22</sup> "But the father said to his servants, 'Quick! Bring the best robe and put it on him. Put a ring on his finger and sandals on his feet. <sup>23</sup> Bring the fattened calf and kill it. Let's have a feast and celebrate. <sup>24</sup> For this son of mine was dead and is alive again; he was lost and is found.' So they began to celebrate.

<sup>25</sup> "Meanwhile, the older son was in the field. When he came near the house, he heard music and dancing. <sup>26</sup> So he called one of the servants and asked him what was going on. <sup>27</sup> 'Your

*brother has come,' he replied, 'and your father has killed the fattened calf because he has him back safe and sound.'*

*²⁸ "The older brother became angry and refused to go in. So his father went out and pleaded with him. ²⁹ But he answered his father, 'Look! All these years I've been slaving for you and never disobeyed your orders. Yet you never gave me even a young goat so I could celebrate with my friends. ³⁰ But when this son of yours who has squandered your property with prostitutes comes home, you kill the fattened calf for him!'*

*³¹ "'My son,' the father said, 'you are always with me, and everything I have is yours. ³² But we had to celebrate and be glad, because this brother of yours was dead and is alive again; he was lost and is found.'"*

Luke 15:14-32

---

**Pods** | Seed pods from the carob tree, used to feed animals.
**Sinned** | Done wrong; rebelled against.

**Fattened calf** | The best calf, set aside for a special celebration.
**Squandered** | Wasted.

---

1. If you were in the younger brother's position in verses 17-19, what kind of response would you be expecting from your father? What's surprising about the father's response in verse 20?

2. The father forgives his son. But he does much more than that. Given that the father in the story represents God, how else do we see God's lavish goodness reflected in verses 22-25?

3. The older brother thinks of himself as a very good person who always obeys his father (verse 29). What kind of person does that turn him into? (See verses 28-30.)

4. The father tells the older brother in verse 31, "You are always with me, and everything I have is yours". Although the older brother already knows this, he's still angry (verses 28-30). Clearly his father's love isn't enough for him. As his sense of fulfilment isn't rooted in his father's love, where *is* it rooted?

5. At the beginning of the story, where does the younger brother look for fulfilment? By the end of the story, where does he find it?

6. Both brothers needed the father's forgiveness: one for his immorality and one for his "morality". What do we learn from the younger brother about how to approach God? And what do we learn from the older brother about how *not* to approach God?

**7. (If time) What has been most striking for you during this session?**

# SESSION 6
# THE LIFE-GIVING GOD

▷ **Celebrity Part 1**

💬 **What, if you lost it, would make you feel that life wasn't worth living?**

*3 What I received I passed on to you as of first importance: that Christ died for our sins according to the Scriptures, 4 that he was buried, that he was raised on the third day according to the Scriptures, 5 and that he appeared to Cephas, and then to the Twelve. 6 After that, he appeared to more than five hundred of the brothers and sisters at the same time, most of whom are still living, though some have fallen asleep. 7 Then he appeared to James, then to all the apostles, 8 and last of all he appeared to me also.*

1 Corinthians 15:3-8

---

**Christ** | Jesus.
**Sins** | Putting anything or anyone in God's rightful place.
**Scriptures** | The Old Testament part of the Bible.
**Raised** | Brought from death to life.
**Cephas** | Another name for Peter.
**The Twelve** | Jesus' twelve closest followers, often called the disciples.

**Brothers and sisters** | Fellow Christians.
**Fallen asleep** | Died.
**James** | One of the twelve disciples.
**Apostles** | "Apostle" means "one sent as a messenger". The apostles were sent by Jesus to tell the world about him.

## ▷ Celebrity Part 2

- If we trust in anything other than God for our ultimate security, we will "die a million deaths" before we actually die.

- When we live for power, approval, comfort or control, then when we don't get those things, we feel as if life isn't worth living.

- These "gods" we live for promise us life, but they can't deliver us from death.

- Jesus demonstrated that he *can* deliver us from death. He proved that by actually overcoming death himself.

- Jesus' resurrection delivers us, not just from "literal" death, but also from the "million deaths" we will suffer before we die if we've put our trust in power, approval, comfort or control.

- A person can only stop trusting these idols if their desire for something else is greater. We need to see Jesus Christ as more desirable to us than anything else.

📖 *²² "People of Athens! I see that in every way you are very religious. ²³ For as I walked around and looked carefully at your objects of worship, I even found an altar with this inscription: 'To an unknown god'. So you are ignorant of the very thing you worship – and this is what I am going to proclaim to you.*

*²⁴ "The God who made the world and everything in it is the Lord of heaven and earth and does not live in temples built by human hands. ²⁵ And he is not served by human hands, as if he needed anything. Rather, he himself gives everyone life and breath and everything else. ²⁶ From one man he made all the nations, that they should inhabit the whole earth; and he marked out their appointed times in history and the boundaries of their lands. ²⁷ God did this so that they would seek him and perhaps reach out for him and find him, though he is not far from any one of us. ²⁸ 'For in him we live and move and have our being.' As some of your own poets have said, 'We are his offspring.'*

*²⁹ "Therefore since we are God's offspring, we should not think that the divine being is like gold or silver or stone – an image made by human design and skill. ³⁰ In the past God overlooked such ignorance, but now he commands all people everywhere to repent. ³¹ For he has set a day when he will judge the world with justice by the man he has appointed. He has given proof of this to everyone by raising him from the dead."*

Acts 17:22-31

---

**Religious** | Devoted to a god or gods.
**Proclaim** | Announce/tell.
**Offspring** | Children and descendants.
**The divine being** | God
**Repent** | To turn away from sin and turn back to God.

---

1. In verse 22 Paul says, "I see that in every way you are very religious". From your own experience, do you think "non-religious" or "anti-religious" people can be religious?

2. Paul then compares the real God with the false gods that people worship instead. Who is the real "Lord of heaven and earth", according to the first bit of verse 24? How is this God different to their idols, according to the end of verse 24?

3. What's the other difference between God and idols, according to verse 25?

4. From what you've heard in this session, how do you think the following idols "need" to be served?

• physical beauty

• approval of others

• money

5. The resurrection shows that, in Christ, we can have life after death. Look again at verse 31. What else does the resurrection show?

6. If we've come to realize that we've been serving idols rather than "the God who made the world and everything in it" (verse 24), what must we do, according to verse 30? What would it take for you to do this?

7. (If time) What has been most striking for you during this session?

# SESSION 7
# THE JOYFUL GOD

▷ **Space Part 1**

≡ What's the best gift God could give you?

¹ Then I saw "a new heaven and a new earth," for the first heaven and the first earth had passed away, and there was no longer any sea. ² I saw the Holy City, the new Jerusalem, coming down out of heaven from God, prepared as a bride beautifully dressed for her husband. ³ And I heard a loud voice from the throne saying, "Look! God's dwelling-place is now among the people, and he will dwell with them. They will be his people, and God himself will be with them and be their God. ⁴ 'He will wipe every tear from their eyes. There will be no more death' or mourning or crying or pain, for the old order of things has passed away."

⁵ He who was seated on the throne said, "I am making everything new!" Then he said, "Write this down, for these words are trustworthy and true."

⁶ He said to me: "It is done. I am the Alpha and the Omega, the Beginning and the End. To the thirsty I will give water without cost from the spring of the water of life. ⁷ Those who are victorious will inherit all this, and I will be their God and they will be my children."

Revelation 21:1-7

**Holy City** | Jerusalem.
**Dwell** | Live.
**The old order of things** | How things used to be.

**Alpha and Omega** | The first and last letters in the Greek alphabet.

▷ **Space Part 2**

- There is, inside each one of us, a longing for relationship, and a longing for home.

- And yet our earthly relationships and our earthly homes never fully satisfy – not even the best ones.

- That's because we were made for another world. The Bible calls it "a new heaven and a new earth" (Revelation 21:1) – a world, real and physical, where we experience both the relationship and the home we've longed for all our lives.

- This new world is described as being like a joyful wedding between Jesus Christ (the bridegroom) and his people (the bride).

- Jesus speaks of those who are shut out from the new heaven and new earth because of their idolatry. As with any wedding, not everyone will be there.

- If you're not living for Christ, which god are you living for instead? Does it give you lasting freedom, fulfilment or peace? Does it have an answer to death? Has it laid down its life for you? Is your god as good as this God has shown himself to be?

2 *"The kingdom of heaven is like a king who prepared a wedding banquet for his son. ³ He sent his servants to those who had been invited to the banquet to tell them to come, but they refused to come.*

⁴ *"Then he sent some more servants and said, 'Tell those who have been invited that I have prepared my dinner: my oxen and fattened cattle have been slaughtered, and everything is ready. Come to the wedding banquet.'*

⁵ *"But they paid no attention and went off – one to his field, another to his business. ⁶ The rest seized his servants, ill-treated them and killed them. ⁷ The king was enraged. He sent his army and destroyed those murderers and burned their city.*

⁸ *"Then he said to his servants, 'The wedding banquet is ready, but those I invited did not deserve to come. ⁹ So go to the street corners and invite to the banquet anyone you find.' ¹⁰ So the servants went out into the streets and gathered all the people they could find, the bad as well as the good, and the wedding hall was filled with guests.*

¹¹ *"But when the king came in to see the guests, he noticed a man there who was not wearing wedding clothes. ¹² He asked, 'How did you get in here without wedding clothes, friend?' The man was speechless.*

¹³ *"Then the king told the attendants, 'Tie him hand and foot, and throw him outside, into the darkness, where there will be weeping and gnashing of teeth.'*

*¹⁴ "For many are invited, but few are chosen."*

Matthew 22:2-14

---

**Kingdom of heaven** | The place where God's people live joyfully under God's rule.
**Wedding clothes** | In those days it was the custom to give wedding guests particular clothes to wear to the banquet.
**Gnashing** | Grinding.

---

1. The king invites guests to his son's wedding banquet three times. He is persistent, patient and generous. What are the different ways in which the invited guests respond in verses 3, 5 and 6?

2. The king in Jesus' story represents God. In verses 7-10, the king responds to this treason in two ways. What are they?

3. In verse 13, a man is thrown out of the wedding banquet.
   Why?

4. Isaiah 61:10 says:

   *"I delight greatly in the LORD;*
   *my soul rejoices in my God.*
   *For he has clothed me with garments of salvation*
   *and arrayed me in a robe of his righteousness."*

   What do you think the "wedding clothes" might
   represent in Jesus' story, and where do they come from?

5. Given what we've learned about God's character during *Life Explored*, why do you think God offers people salvation, and how has he made that possible?

6. If you had to cast yourself in this story, which one of these four characters would you be?

   Do you see other things as more valuable to you than being at the Son's banquet (verse 5)?

   Would you consider yourself to be hostile to the invitation (verse 6)?

   Do you feel you're already acceptable to God, without needing the "wedding clothes" he provides (verse 11)?

   Or would you accept the invitation to the Son's wedding banquet?

7. (If time) What has been most striking for you during this session?

Keep exploring at your own pace by visiting
**www.life.explo.red**.